Guitar: The First 100 Chords for Guitar

How to Learn and Play Guitar Chords: The Complete Beginner Guitar Method

ISBN: 978-1-911267-98-0

Published by **www.fundamental-changes.com**

www.fundamental-changes.com

Twitter: **@guitar_joseph**
Over 7500 fans on Facebook: **FundamentalChangesInGuitar**
Instagram: **FundamentalChanges**

For over 250 Free Guitar Lessons with Videos Check Out
www.fundamental-changes.com

Cover Image Copyright: Shutterstock: _EG_ / Brian A Jackson

Other Books from Fundamental Changes

Contents

Get the Audio

The audio files for this book are available to download for free from **www.fundamental-changes.com.** The link is in the top right-hand corner. Simply select this book title from the drop-down menu and follow the instructions to get the audio.

We recommend that you download the files directly to your computer, not to your tablet, and extract them there before adding them to your media library. You can then put them on your tablet, iPod or burn them to CD. On the download page there is a help PDF, and we also provide technical support via the contact form.

For over 250 Free Guitar Lessons with Videos Check out:
www.fundamental-changes.com

Twitter: **@guitar_joseph**
Over 7500 fans on Facebook: **FundamentalChangesInGuitar**
Instagram: **FundamentalChanges**

Get your audio now for free:

It makes the book come alive, and you'll learn much more!

www.fundamental-changes.com/download-audio

Introduction

The first chords you learn on guitar may take you some time. Not only are you learning to use your fingers in a completely new way, you also have to learn some intricate muscle movements and commit those to subconscious memory. If you're a musician, or have ever played a sport, you may have heard the term 'muscle memory'.

Muscle memory is the name for something that is so automated that we no longer have to think about it. Walking, riding a bike, throwing a ball and swimming are all examples of processes where we need to develop muscle memory to do them well. They are all *learned* processed which may have taken some time for you to develop (probably when you were very young), but once you know them, the movements go to a very deep part of your brain and you don't need to actively think about them to make them work.

In fact, if you tried to think about the exact sequence of muscles you need to trigger in order to walk, then you would never get anywhere at all!

Walking probably took you a good few months to figure out, but now you probably never think about having to do it at all. Remember this fact while you're taking your first steps on guitar. For many people, playing chords isn't an instant skill and it will take a while before their precise movements are committed muscle memory. To put chords firmly into muscle memory we need to do a bit of structured (yet fun!) practice, where we train our brains exactly how to form each chord, and how to move from one chord to another.

Chords need to be locked into our muscle memory because we don't have a lot of time to form, or change between them when playing songs. If we change too slowly there will be a big hole in the rhythm and flow of the song. To use a sporting analogy again; imagine what would happen if you had to actually think about blocking every time someone threw a punch in a boxing match. We need to build chords to the point where they become a reflex reaction.

Developing this skill isn't as hard as it may seem… It just takes a bit of commitment, regular practice and a structured approach to learning. As adults, we sometimes don't like to learn new things. It's easy to feel that learning finished when we left school or college, so we can sometimes shy away from new challenges or experiences. Music, however, is a really fun habit to get into. The results can be quick and effortless, or sometimes slow and challenging. Either way, the end result; playing music, is one of the most rewarding experiences you can have.

If you want to use this book as a reference, you can dive straight in now. However, in the final chapters I have included some really useful tips on how to practice efficiently, develop some great playing habits that will stay with you for life, and move from learning chords to playing songs by adding rhythm. These sections will teach you to learn and memorise chords more quickly, make you into a better musician, and help you develop a healthy approach to the guitar.

Two questions that guitar teachers get asked regularly are:

How long will it take to learn to play the guitar?

And,

How many chords are there?

Both are quite difficult to answer.

The first is difficult to answer because it has a lot of variables. For example, how much will you practice? Will you focus on the right things? *How* will you practice? How do you define 'being able to play the guitar'? – Do you just want to strum a few chords around a campfire or is it your goal to become the next Eddie Van Halen?

With all these variables and more, it is almost impossible to give a straight answer or time frame. But, if you practice for about twenty minutes every day, practice efficiently and are aiming to play some chord-based pop music, then it normally takes a few months to get fairly competent.

In answer to the second question, the answer is simply 'lots, but as a guitarist you will probably use relatively few of them'. Luckily for us, once you've learned a few 'open' chords and a few 'barre' chords, you can play pretty much any chord or song on the guitar.

Let's get started and look at the *open position* chords available to us. If you're a beginner, I highly recommend working through Chapter One in conjunction with the How to Practice section at the end of the book.

A Final Note!

PLEASE download and listen to the audio along with each example. It will really help you develop as a player. It takes a lot longer to reach a goal if you don't know what that goal looks (or sounds) like.

Get the audio examples from **www.fundamental-changes.com** and follow the instructions. The Download Audio tab is in the top right.

How to Read Chord Diagrams

The following images show how the written notation of a chord diagram relates to where you place your fingers on the neck of a guitar to play a chord. Pay careful attention to which strings are played and which fingers are use.

The first diagram shows the notes on each of the open strings of the guitar.

The second diagram shows you how to number the fingers of the fretting hand. If you are left-handed, the same numbers apply to your right hand

The third diagram shows the standard way chords are notated on chord *girds*. Each dot represents where you place a finger.

The final diagram shows how the notation relates to where you place your fingers on the guitar neck.

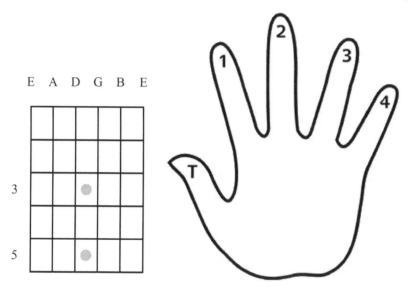

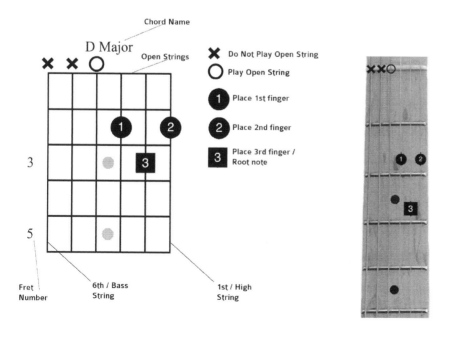

Chapter One: Open Position Chords

Open position chords are normally the first chords people learn on the guitar. They are named 'open position' chords because they often use open strings as notes within the chord. As you will see later, there are many chords which do not use open strings.

Open position chords can be used to play the majority of songs that you hear on the radio (depending on your taste in music!). They are great to use while songwriting because they are relatively easy to play, and provide a 'full-sounding' harmony to accompany vocals or other instruments.

Not all chords are easily accessible in the open position, but songs are written by guitarists are normally in easy 'guitar keys', so you will find that the chords in this chapter cover most situations.

The first chord I teach my students is normally E Minor, or 'Em' for short. It looks like this as a chord diagram:

Example 1a:

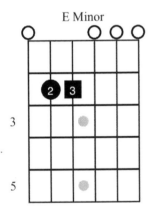

The root of the E Minor chord is the note 'E' and is played on the lowest open string (the thickest bass string). Look at how the above diagram relates to the neck image on the previous page.

Place your second finger on the 2nd fret of the 5th string, and then place your third finger on the 2nd fret of the 4th string, right next to it.

Make sure you use the correct fingers; it's tempting to use the first and second finger, but they will be needed a little later. Refer to the hand diagram on the previous page if you're not sure.

Now flick to the **How to Practice** section and work through the first set of exercises for learning new chords. Apply these steps to the Em chord.

Let's learn our second chord: A Minor, or Am.

Am is played like this.

Example 1b:

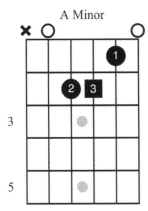

A Minor

Notice that there is an 'x' on the bottom string of the guitar, so do *not* play it. Strum the guitar from the 5th string downwards.

Compare the notes and fingering of Am to Em. Can you see that the second and third fingers both move across one string as a single unit and then the first finger is added on the second string?

Complete the steps in the **How to Practice** section and work with a metronome up to the target speed.

A quick note about your thumb

The thumb of the fretting hand should be placed on the back of the neck, roughly in line with the fingers but not necessarily directly behind them. This placement isn't a precise science, but the thumb provides support for the fretting fingers to squeeze against. Sometimes, the thumb may be closer to the head of the guitar than the fingers and it will normally find a slightly different position for each chord. As long as the hand is comfortable and each note rings clearly you should be fine.

Be aware though, if you're just starting out playing guitar, you'll probably have a tendency to 'over-squeeze' the neck when playing chords. Experiment with the smallest possible pressure you can use to play the chord cleanly. Fret the chord, and make sure that when you strum it, each note rings. Then simply relax the pressure gradually in your hand to find the minimum pressure needed to make the chord ring out.

When you feel confident playing both Em and Am separately, work through the steps in the **Learning Chords in Context section** of the **How to Practice** chapter, and learn how to combine the two chords together as a short piece of music.

Next, add some strumming to the chord progression using steps in Chapter Thirteen.

Listen for any buzzes and muted notes while you play each chord and try to minimise these as much as possible.

The next chord to learn is C Major. Notice that it has two fretted notes in common with Am. All you need to do to move from Am to C Major is move your third finger off the 3rd string, and on to the 3rd fret on the 5th string. This is a bit of a stretch at first, but adjust your thumb position on the back of the neck, and you will soon find a comfortable way to play the chord. Start your strum from the fifth string and avoid the sixth.

Example 1c:

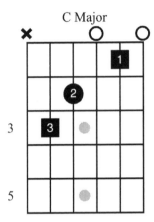

Compare the chords of Am and C Major to see how much they have in common. Use the steps in the **How to Practice** section learn the chord of C Major and then link it with the chord of Am.

The next chord to learn is D Major. Pay attention to the fingering and listen to the audio track so you can hear how it should sound.

Example 1d:

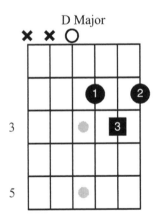

Learn D Major just as you learnt the previous three chords. First tackle it individually and build your muscle memory, then work through the steps to combine it with another chord. I recommend you combine it with Em to begin with.

G Major is a little harder because it uses all four fingers. Listen to the audio and practice matching the sound you hear. Be careful to pay attention to any buzzes or muted noted you create.

Example 1e:

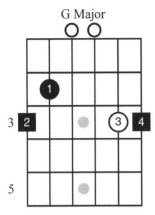

G Major

The white note is optional. If you decide not to play it, that's fine, but it's good to know it is an option.

Work through the steps to incorporate this chord into your vocabulary. I recommend that you pair G Major with Em for now. G Major is a challenging chord and Em is less difficult. If you really can't manage to play between G Major and Em in rhythm, simply strum on the open strings instead of the Em. It won't sound great, but it will help you build muscle memory on the G Major before adding the Em back into the sequence.

Our brains work best when learning new information in context, so practicing pairs of chords helps us learn the muscle memory of the chord change, as well as the chord's sound, feel, and how it works in relation to other chords.

The following sets of chords are good to learn in pairs. Learn each one individually at first and then use the steps in the **How to Practice** section to build your muscle memory and fluency as you combine them. Some new chords are paired with chords you already know.

Example 1f:

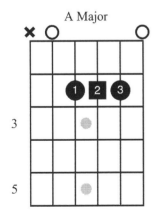
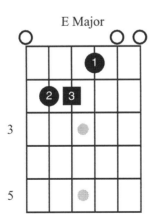

A Major   E Major

Example 1g:

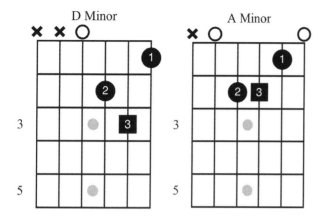

The next chord, F Major, is challenging as it uses a small *barre* to play two notes on the 1st fret. Getting a barre right is all about the position of your *thumb* (believe it or not!). Until now, your thumb has been placed towards the top of half of the neck and used to squeeze against the fretting fingers. With the F Major chord, experiment by allowing your thumb to drop right down to the bottom half of the guitar neck. This movement will rotate your wrist slightly and make it easier to get your first finger parallel to the fret wire to play the barre.

Learn F Major in conjunction with A Minor.

Example 1h:

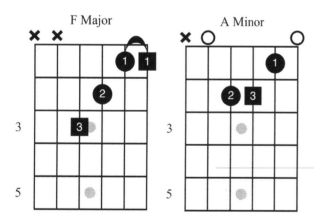

F Major is one of the more difficult chords, so if you are struggling it's ok to play the easier chord of F Major 7 (FMaj7). Instead of the barre, you can play the first string open.

Example 1i:

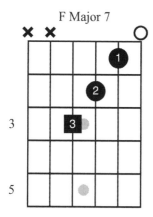

Test yourself and make some music!

After you have worked through the steps in the **How to Practice** section, try the following short chord progressions. You don't have to know all the chords in this chapter before you begin… just work with what you have. Add new chords as you learn them and get creative with your practice. Some chords sound better together than others, and trial and error is a great way to discover new and exciting sounds.

Example 1j:

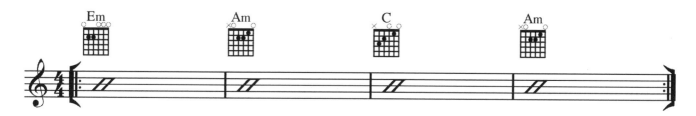

Example 1k:

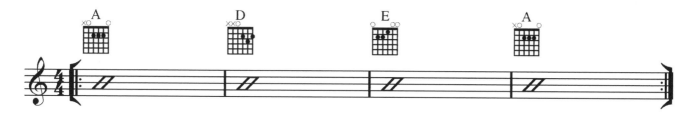

Example 1l:

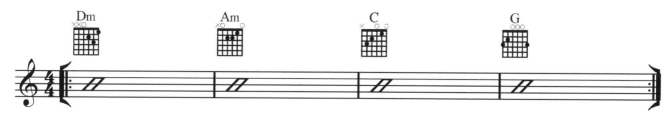

Example 1m:

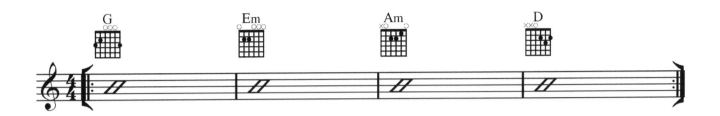

Example 1n:

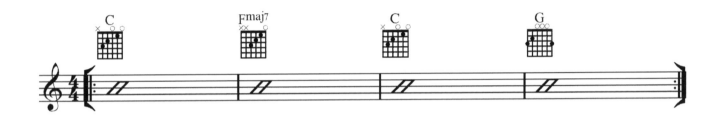

You'll probably begin by just strumming one chord per bar of music, but as you work further through the **How to Practice** section, start adding more rhythms and strumming patterns. There's a breakdown of how to strum rhythms on the guitar in **Chapter Thirteen**.

Think about *how* you play each chord… loud or soft? Gentle or Aggressive? Pick or no pick?

The most important thing to do is listen carefully to what you play. Don't accept any muted notes or buzzes! Keep adjusting your fingers and thumb until each chord is clean! If you need to, go back to the muscle memory exercises on individual chords and make sure you are placing your fingers correctly

If your fingers get sore, take a break and come back later.

Have fun! – You're making music.

Chapter Two: Dominant 7 Open Chords

The chords in this section are named *Dominant 7* chords. They have a slightly tense sound and often want to *resolve* that *tension* to another chord. These chords will expand your musical horizons and teach you some great new sounds.

As always, learn these chords in pairs. Combine a chord you don't know with one that you do, then practice moving between them. Each new chord is listed with a suggested friend you learnt in Chapter One.

Example 2a:

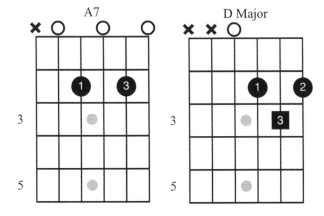

Example 2b:

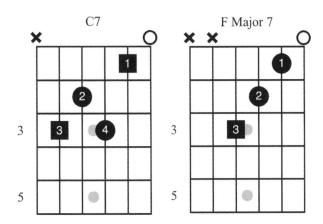

Example 2c:

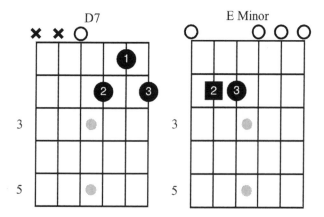

Example 2d:

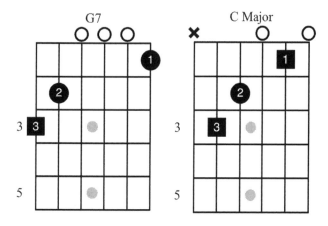

Example 2e: *On the B7, the second string can also be played open.*

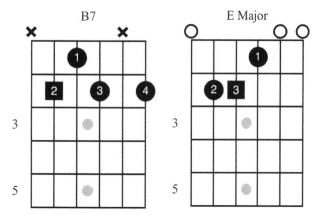

Example 2f:

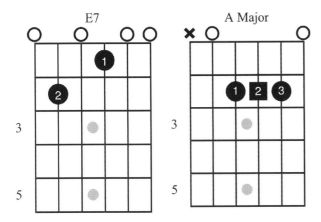

Test yourself!

Once you have introduced each new chord into your vocabulary by using the steps in the **How to Practice** section, work towards building the following short chord progressions. Begin by strumming one chord per bar and gradually add more interesting rhythms by working through **Chapter Thirteen.**

Example 2g:

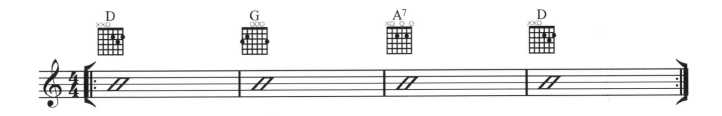

Example 2h:

Example 2i:

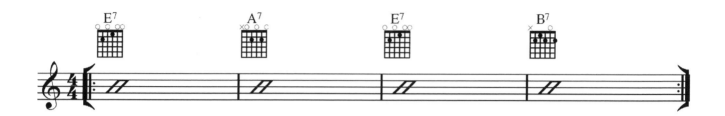

Example 2j:

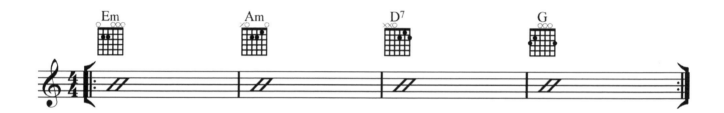

Example 2k:

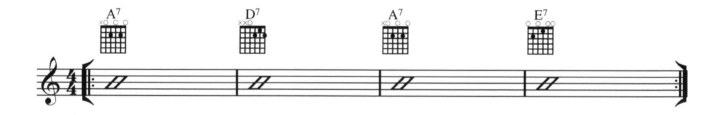

Chapter Three: Barre Chords

We will look at some more open chords in Chapter Five, but first it's time to learn some essential *barre* chords.

A barre chord uses a finger to make a bar (*barre* in Spanish, the birthplace of the guitar) across multiple strings. You saw a mini-barre in Chapter One in the chord of F Major. Now, however, we will learn to use a full-barre to form some new and important chord shapes.

Barre chords have an advantage over open chords: They're movable. It is possible to slide a barre chord up and down the strings to play different chords because barre chords don't contain any open strings.

For example, play an E Minor chord, then slide your fingers up one fret and strum the chord again. It sounds wrong because you moved some of the notes (the fretted ones) up the neck, but the notes on the open strings stayed put. If we could bring the open string with us when we move the chord up the neck, we could keep the relationship between all the notes the same and 'not leave any notes behind'.

Barre chords allow us to bring the open strings with us as we move chord shapes around the neck.

The first barre chord to learn is the 'minor' barre. Compare the barre chord version of Bm below, with the open position chord of Em.

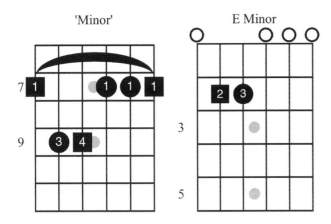

Can you see that these two chords are formed identically? The barre in the first diagram replaces the open strings in the second Em diagram.

The first chord hasn't been named, although when you place the barre at the 7th fret this just happens to be a Bm because the note at the 7th fret of the sixth string is B. We will look at this in more detail soon.

For now, practice forming the chord of Bm by placing your first finger across the strings at the 7th fret and using your third and fourth fingers to play the other notes.

Example 3a:

'Minor'

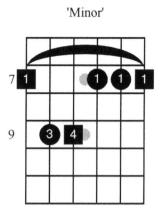

Playing a barre is tricky at first. Just as with the F Major chord in Chapter One, a big part of the secret is to move your thumb to the lower half of the neck. However, it is also important to place the barre finger on its *side* so that the nail of the finger *points towards the head of the guitar.*

If you place the finger so the nail points in the same direction as the fret wire, you will find that the strings fall into the little folds of your finger joints and become muted. By using the *bony side* of the finger, you will make a better contact with the strings and your chords will sound much cleaner.

Barre chords are always a challenge for beginners, but with a little perseverance and some analytic practice, you will get the knack of it in no time.

Work through the **How to Practice** steps to commit the barre chord to muscle memory. Don't worry if this takes a few days or weeks! Try combining it with an Em or a strum on open strings to help you master the movement.

The shape you have just learnt is a Minor barre chord with its root on the *sixth* string. Notice that the square root marker is on the lowest string of the guitar. The chord written above is a B Minor chord because the root has been placed on the note B. If you know the names of the notes on the bottom string of the guitar, you can place this chord shape anywhere and play *any* minor chord.

Here are the notes on the bottom string of the guitar:

Notes on the Sixth String

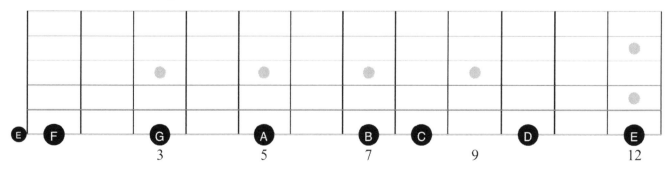

So, by placing the minor barre on the 5th fret, you will create an Am chord:

Example 3b:

A Minor

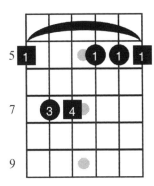

If you place the minor barre shape on the 10th fret, you will play a Dm chord.

Example 3c:

D Minor

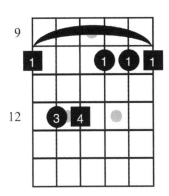

Check that these chords sound similar to their open string versions by first playing the barre chord and then playing the open string chord. The *voicing* of the chord is different, but they both have the same overall sound or *tonality*.

Example 3d:

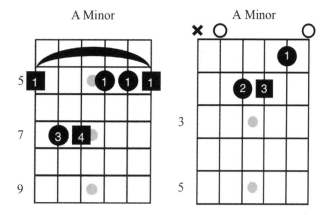

Use the map of the notes on the sixth string above to play the following chord progression. All you need to do is use the minor barre shape and slide to the correct location for each chord. Listen to the audio to hear how this works.

Example 3e:

The note Bb is located on the 6th fret between A and B

Now you have learnt the Minor barre chord voicing for the sixth string, let's learn the *Major* barre chord voicing.

Example 3f:

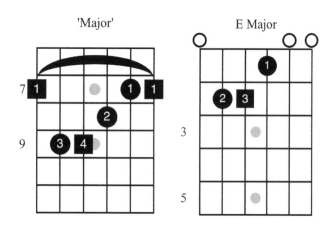

As you can see, this barre chord has the same shape as the open E Major chord from Chapter One, but it uses a first finger barre instead of playing the open strings:

Barre chords allow us to move all the notes in a chord up the neck while keeping their relationship with the root intact. Everything moves in the same amount because there are no open strings.

All we need, is to know a barre shape for each chord *type* (major, minor '7' etc.), and where to place it.

Repeat example 3e, but this time use major barres instead of minor barres.

Example 3g:

We can also play barre chords on the fifth string using the A Major, and A Minor shapes from Chapter One.

Here is a movable Minor barre chord shape with the root on the fifth string.

Example 3h:

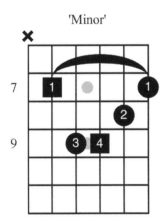

Here is the movable Major barre chord shape with the root on the fifth string.

Example 3i:

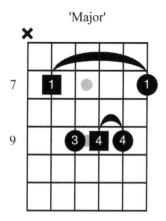

'Major'

The major barre on the 5th string is quite challenging because the barre is not played with the first finger. In fact, there are various ways to finger this chord; some people even play all three notes on the 9th fret with a third finger barre. Either way, you don't need to worry about hitting the note on the 1st (thinnest) string. It's a bit awkward and doesn't add much to the sound of the chord so don't worry if it is muted for now.

Once you know how to play the Major and Minor barre chord shapes on the fifth string, all you need to know is where to find the root notes to be able to access *any* major or minor chord. The following diagram shows the location of each note on the fifth string. Notes like D#/Eb are located between the notes D and E.

Notes on the Fifth String

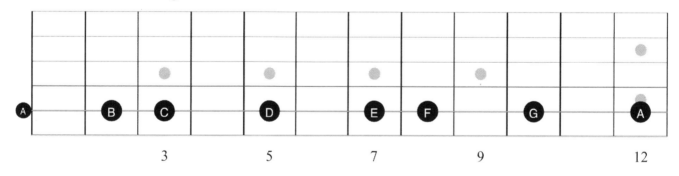

Play through the following sequence using only minor barre chords on the fifth string.

Example 3j:

Cm   Ebm   Fm   Gm

Play through the following sequence using only major barre chords on the fifth string.

Example 3k:

Play through the following sequence but this time combine major and minor barre chords on the fifth string.

Example 3l:

Next, play through this progression that combines major and minor barres on both the 5th and the 6th strings. There are a few ways to play this progression depending on where you choose to play the barres. You could play any chord with a root on either the 5th or 6th string.

Example 3m:

Try playing through some of the progressions in Chapters One and Two but this time play them with barre chords.

The placement of barre chords can be limited by the type of guitar you are playing. It is more difficult to play barres on an acoustic guitar as the strings are normally thicker. Also, acoustic guitars often only tend to give access to around the 10th fret where the guitar neck joins the body.

Electric guitars usually have a greater available range and thinner strings, making barre chords easier to play.

There are barre chord shapes for every type of chord *quality*. We will talk more about chord qualities and look at a little theory in the next chapter, but for now, simply learn the following barre chord shapes.

Example 3n:

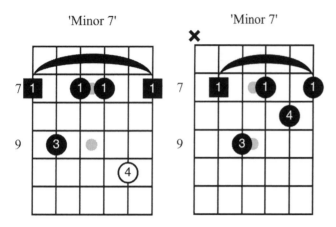

Example 3o:

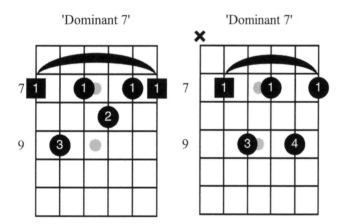

Example 3p:

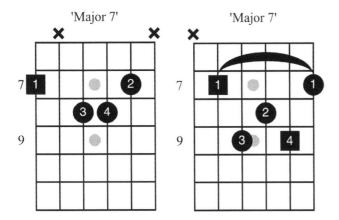

Even though the Major 7 barre on the sixth string isn't technically a barre chord, the underside of the first finger is used to mute the unfretted fifth string as shown by the 'x'. As there are no ringing strings, the shape is movable.

As always, learn each barre chord individually using the steps in the **How to Practice** chapter, before combining different chords into sequences.

Here are some ideas to get you started. It doesn't matter whether you use a 6th string, or a 5th string barre to play each chord so there are many ways to play through each sequence. Try to keep the chords close together to avoid big movements up and down the neck. For example, it is normally preferable to play Am to Dm by moving a barre chord from the 6th to the 5th string, than by sliding the same shape from the 5th to the 10th fret on the sixth string.

Example 3q:

Example 3r:

Example 3s:

Try altering sequences from the previous two chapters to use these new 7th chords. Try turning a Major chord into a Dominant 7 or a Major 7th. Try turning a Minor chord into a m7 chord or a Dominant 7th. You can create some great results.

Write down your favourite ideas and you'll be well on your way to some serious song writing.

Chapter Four: A Little (Non-Scary) Music Theory

If you're *not* interested in learning the theory of how music works, and just want to learn some more chords then you are allowed to skip this chapter! I do suggest you use this section as a little 'light' night time reading though because it's good to understand what you are playing; it will help you to be more creative.

In previous chapters, we came across some '7th' chords so let's now learn how they are formed.

Chord construction begins with scales.

What is a scale?

As far as we need to know for this book, a scale is a sequence of notes that begins and ends in the same place. For example, the scale of C Major is

C D E F G A B C

Scales are very important, so if you want more information about how they work, I highly recommend my two books, The Circle of Fifths for Guitarists and **The Practical Guide to Modern Music Theory for Guitarists**.

What is a chord?

A chord, technically, is the combination of three or more notes. A major or minor chord has only three individual notes. Often, major or minor chords on the guitar *look* like they have more than three notes. However, even though we play notes on four, five, or even six strings, we are only actually playing three separate individual notes which are doubled in different octaves.

For example, in the following chord of C Major, the names of the notes are labelled... You can see that even though we play six strings, there are only three unique notes.

C Major Chord

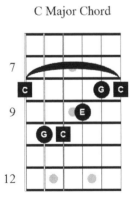

In this voicing, the note C appears three times, and the note G appears twice. The only note to appear once is the E.

Where do these notes come from?

To find out which notes go together to form each individual chord, we must learn how to *harmonise* the major scale.

Chords are formed when we 'stack' specific notes from a scale on top of each other. Look again at the previous example. The chord of C Major contains *only* the notes, C, E and G. In the context of the major scale, we have taken the notes 1, 3 and 5:

C	D	E	F	G	A	B	C
1	2	3	4	5	6	7	8/1

This can be seen as 'jumping over', or 'leapfrogging' every other note in the scale. For example, we formed this chord by starting on C, Jumping D and landing on E, jumping F and landing on G. This is how most simple, three-note chords are formed.

C E G

D F A

E G B

F A C

G B D

A C E

B D F

If we view the notes of C Major spaced out on the fretboard, we can establish what pattern of notes is required to form A Major chord.

Example 4a:

C Major

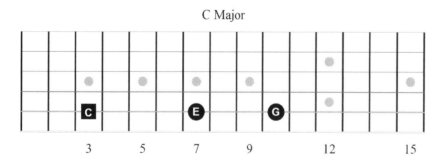

The distance between the notes C and E is *two tones*.

Any chord with a distance of two tones between the first two notes can be classed as a 'major-type' chord. This distance in music is called a *'major 3rd'*.

The distance between the 3rd and 5th (the notes E and G), is *one-and-a-half tones*. This is *one semitone smaller* than the major 3rd, so we call it a *minor* 3rd.

When measured from the *root*, any major chord *must* consist of two tones between the root and 3rd, and three-and-a-half tones between the root and 5th.

It is the convention in music to describe the notes in a chord in terms of their relationship to the major scale formula, **1 2 3 4 5 6 7**.

So, in simple terms, a Major chord has the formula 1 3 5, and **the first chord of any major scale is always major.**

Moving on to the second note in the C Major scale, (D) and repeating the previous process we generate:

C	D	E	F	G	A	B	C
1	2	3	4	5	6	7	8/1

As we harmonise up from the second note of the scale, we get the notes D, F and A. On the guitar, these look and sounds like:

Example 4b:

D Minor

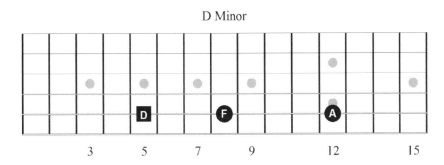

The distance between the notes D and F is one-and-a-half tones or a '*minor 3rd*' which means that the chord is *minor*.

However; the distance between the notes D and A is still three-and-a-half tones, which is the correct spacing for a *perfect* 5th.

With a minor 3rd and a perfect 5th, this chord is classified as a minor chord built on the note D, or simply 'D minor' for short.

As a formula, a minor chord is expressed as 1 b3 5 and **the second chord in any major key is always minor.**

All the notes of the major scale can be harmonised in this way, and with the exception of the 7th note, B, they are all major or minor chords.

To save space, I will not show the construction of every chord (although do try this by yourself). The harmonised chords of the C Major scale are:

Chord I	C Major
Chord ii	D Minor
Chord iii	E Minor
Chord IV	F Major
Chord V	G Major
Chord vi	A Minor
Chord vii	B Minor (b5) or B *Diminished*

It is quite rare to play a Diminished chord, so we won't cover them here. In the table above, you will see that instead of listing each chord 1, 2, 3, etc., they are listed by Roman numerals. This may seem strange but actually saves a lot of confusion later. Major chords are shown with capital letters, and Minor chords are shown with lower case letters.

Chords I, IV, and V are Major

Chords ii, iii, vi and vii are Minor.

7th Chords

In Chapter Three, we studied Dominant 7 chords.

In music, you will sometimes see chords with names like 'G7', 'A minor 7', 'C Major 7' or even 'B minor 7b5'. All these '7th' chords can be formed from the major scale. In fact, they are simply *extensions* to the original process we used to construct chords in the harmonisation chapters.

Look back at how we formed major and minor chords from the major scale. We took the first, third and fifth notes by leapfrogging adjacent scale tones. If we continue to jump notes to land on the seventh note, i.e., 1 3 5 **7** we would have created a '7th' chord. For example:

C	D	E	F	G	A	B	C
1	2	3	4	5	6	7	8/1

In addition to the notes C, E, and G, we have now introduced the note B. This chord is a C Major *triad* with an added *natural 7th* and is named C Major 7. Notice how the 7th note, (B) is *one semitone* below the root, (C). The chord can be played like this:

Example 4c:

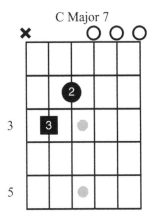

C Major 7

The added note, B is played on the open 2nd string. Play and listen to this chord. Notice how it has a richness compared to an ordinary C Major chord. The formula for A Major 7th chord is 1 3 5 7.

When we add the 7th note to chord ii (D minor), we get the following notes:

D F A C.

This time, the 7th note (C) is a *whole tone* below the root, (D). This 7th note, therefore, is a *b7* not a *natural 7* as in the previous example of C Major.

When we add a b7 note to a minor chord, the chord is named 'minor 7'. In this case, we have formed the chord of D minor 7. It can be played like this:

Example 4d:

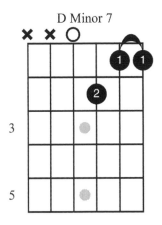

D Minor 7

I hear this as a kind of *softened* minor chord. Still sad, but not as sad as a straight minor chord. Any minor 7 chord has the formula 1 b3 5 b7.

The previous two chord types, major 7 and minor 7, account for five of the harmonised scale tones:

Chord 1 (Imaj7)	C Major 7
Chord 2 (iim7)	D Minor 7
Chord 3 (iiim7)	E Minor 7
Chord 4 (IVmaj7)	F Major 7
Chord 5	
Chord 6 (vim7)	A Minor 7
Chord 7	

As you can see, I have missed out chords V and vii. This is because they are slightly different. As you now know, when we harmonise the major scale, chord V (G) is always A Major chord. However, the added the 7th note *not* a natural 7th. Here is the harmonised V chord in the Key of C:

G B D **F.**

The note F is a whole tone below the root, (G). This is similar to the b7th note in a minor 7 chord. What we now have is a major chord with an added *b7*.

This chord is called a *dominant* 7 and is simply written as a '7' after the chord root, e.g., *G7* or *A7*. It has the formula 1 3 5 b7. G7 can be played like this:

Example 4e:

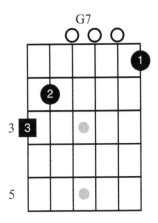

Dominant 7 chords have a tense, unresolved sound, and often move to tonic (home) chord the key, in this case, C Major.

Finally, when we harmonise the 7th note of the major scale, we generate a chord which is fairly uncommon in pop or rock music but is often used in jazz.

Chord vii forms a *minor b5* or *diminished* chord. When we harmonise this chord up to four notes from the key of C, we get

B D F **A**

Again, we are adding a flattened 7th (b7), and so the chord is now described as a 'minor 7b5'. It is often written as *m7b5*. In this case, you would see Bm7b5. This type of chord has the formula 1 b3 b5 b7.

It is played like this and has a dark, brooding quality:

Example 4f:

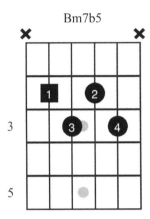

We can now complete the chart of the harmonised major scale.

Chord Imaj7	C Major 7
Chord iim7	D Minor 7
Chord iiim7	E Minor 7
Chord IVmaj7	F Major 7
Chord V7	G7 or G *Dominant* 7
Chord vim7	A Minor 7
Chord viim7b5	B Minor 7 b5 or Bm7b5

You will be very pleased to know there is a simple shorthand way to describe and write any type of 7th chord.

Each has a special formula that describes the way they are formed.

Remember that a major chord has the formula 1 3 5.

A minor chord (with that smaller distance between the 1 and 3) has the formula 1 b3 5.

The following table shows the construction and naming convention of all 7th chords.

Chord	Formula
Major 7 (Maj7)	1 3 5 7
Dominant 7 (7)	1 3 5 b7
Minor 7 (m7)	1 b3 5 b7
Minor 7 flat 5 (m7b5)	1 b3 b5 b7

Major 7 chords are the only chords to have a 'natural' 7th. All other chords (at least for the purposes of this book) have b7s.

To see this process in action, we can simply compare some of the notes in different 'C' chords.

Chord	Formula	Notes
C Major 7	1 3 5 7	C E G B
C7	1 3 5 b7	C E G Bb
Cm7	1 b3 5 b7	C Eb G Bb
Cm7b5	1 b3 b5 b7	C Eb Gb Bb

That's definitely enough theory for now! Let's move on and learn some new chords.

Chapter Five: More Open Chords

We have looked at the most important 7th chords in barre chord form, but there are some really beautiful '7th' voicings you can play in the open position.

Learn the following chords just as you did in the earlier chapters.

Example 5a:

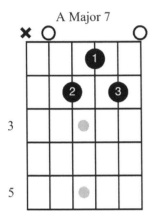

Example 5b:

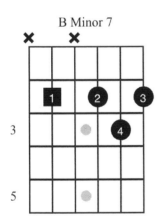

Example 5c:

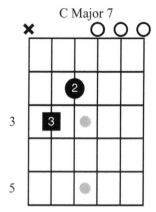

Example 5d:

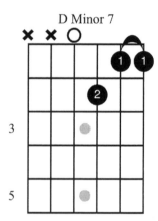

Example 5e:

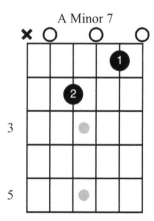

Example 5f:

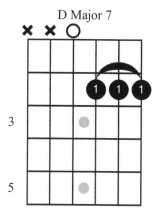

Example 5g:

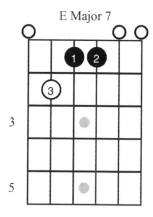

Example 5h:

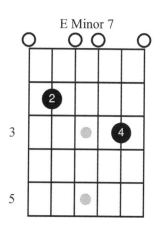

Example 5i:

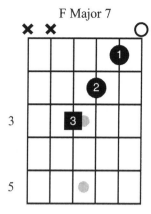

F Major 7

Example 5j:

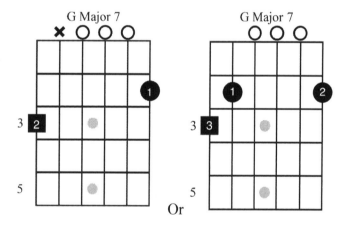

G Major 7   G Major 7

Or

There are also a few chord types we haven't covered yet.

A *suspended or 'sus'* chord is one that replaces the 3rd with either the 2nd or the 4th.

Instead of 1 3 5, the formula is 1 2 5 or 1 4 5.

Instead of C E G, the notes are C D G or C F G.

If the 3rd is replaced with the 2nd, the chord is named 'sus2'. If the 3rd is replaced with the 4th, then the chord is named 'sus4'.

Here are some suspended open chords. Play them and you will hear why they are named 'suspended'.

Example 5k:

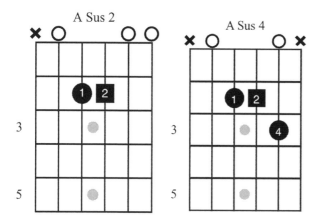

Example 5l:

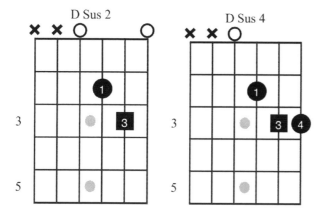

'6' chords have the formula 1 3 5 6. They are quite rich-sounding and a little bit 'jazz'. Often they are used quite sparsely in music as they can quickly overpower a pop-type chord progression.

Example 5m:

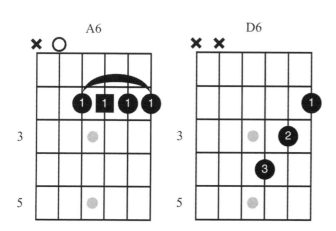

Example 5n:

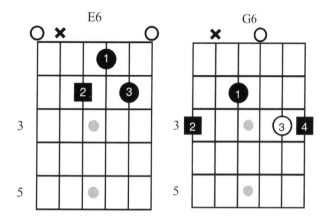

* On the E6, be careful to avoid the fifth string. Try playing the sixth string by itself, then jumping over the fifth string to strum the rest of the chord.

Test Yourself!

Use the following progressions to test your knowledge of the chords in this chapter. Combine these chords with chords that you already know to create new music.

You can also 'substitute' one chord for another. For example, if you see a D Major chord in an earlier chord sequence, try substituting it for a Dsus2, Dsus4, DMaj7 or D7. Not every chord substitution will work, and some might sound kind of weird, but you'll never know until you experiment. Try it; it's fun!

Example 5o:

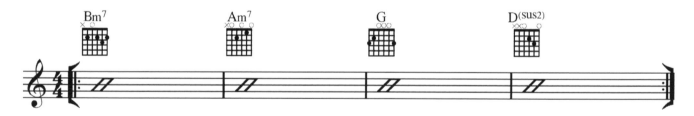

Example 5p:

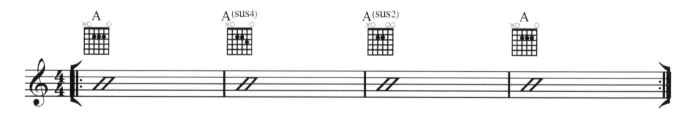

Example 5q:

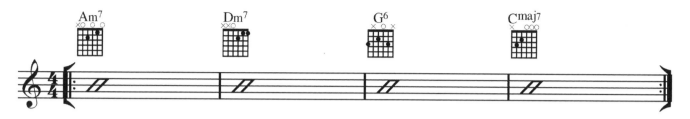

Example 5r:

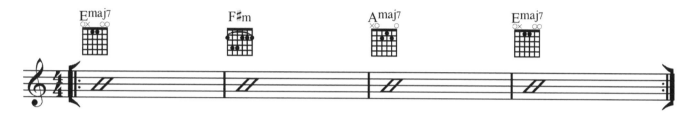

Example 5s:

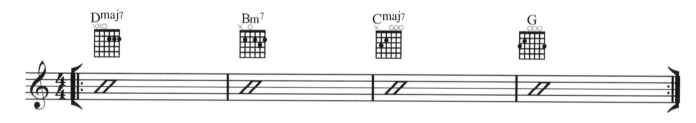

Chapter Six: More Barre Chords

The chords in this chapter are mainly barre chord versions of the Suspended and '6' open chords in Chapter Five. However, we will explore a couple of important '9' chords.

Here are the barre chord voicings of the suspended chords that you should know.

Example 6a: - sixth string root

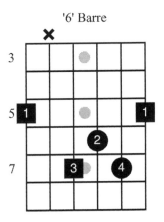

* Be careful to avoid the fifth string

Example 6b: fifth string root

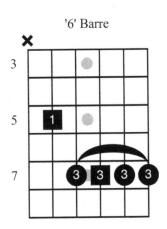

Notice how these barre chord shapes are once again based around the open position versions of the chords.

Next, here are the sus2 and sus 4 voicings you should know. These are normally played as barres on the fifth string.

Example 6c:

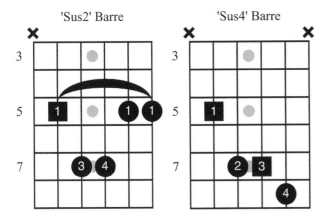

Experiment with the fingering of the Sus4 barre. Many guitarists use a third-finger barre to play the notes on the 3rd and 4th strings.

Next, let's take a quick look at a few common 'Dominant 9' chord voicings.

A Dominant 9 chord is an extension of a Dominant 7 chord and can normally be used as a straight substitution: For example, anywhere you could play a D7 you could play a D9 instead[1].

Building on the ideas in Chapter Four, a Dominant 9 chord is built by extending a Dominant 7 chord by one note.

A Dominant 7 chord is 1 3 5 b7

A Dominant 9 chord is 1 3 5 b7 9

However, we don't normally have to play all the notes of a chord to convey its unique quality. Quite often we will miss out notes like the 5th as they don't really add much to the character of the sound.

Dominant 9 chords are the backbone of most funk tunes, especially anything James Brown-esque. The most common barre chord voicing is this one.

Example 6d:

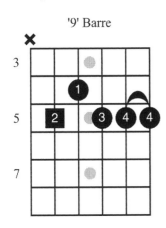

---

[1] Handle with care!

There are a variety of ways to finger the above chord voicing. Many players will barre with their third finger across all three of the top strings.

It's also possible to play a '9' barre chord with a root on the 6th string, but it's a bit awkward and less common.

Example 6e:

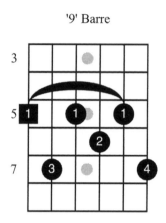

'9' Barre

Personally, I'd avoid playing the notes on the 5th and 6th strings, and just aim to hit the top four strings as much as possible. Often it's OK to let the bass player take care of the root notes so that the guitar doesn't take up too much sonic space in the band. A lot depends on context though. If it's just you and a singer, you'll normally need to play the root notes.

Test yourself!

Work through the following chord progressions using barre chords. To refresh your memory, the root notes on the 6th and 5th strings are given below.

Notes on the Sixth String

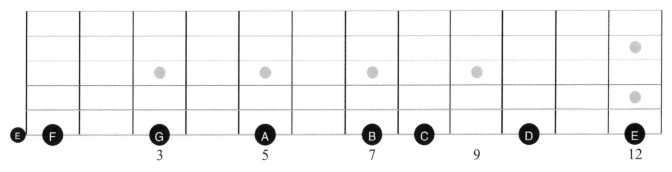

Notes on the Fifth String

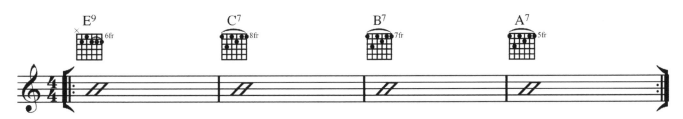

Example 6f:

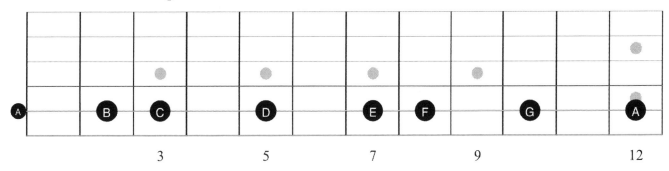

Example 6g:

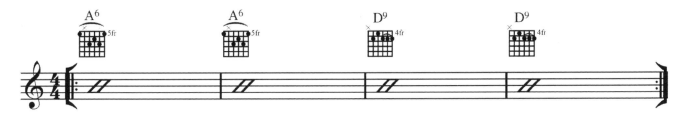

Chapter Seven: Bass Note Movements

When playing open chords, it is common to use small movements in the bass to help link chords smoothly together. The 'top' part of the chord stays the same, but the lowest notes of the chord will often descend or ascend by step. This type of movement is called a *descending bassline*.

It is easy to move between C Major and A Minor by using a descending bassline.

Example 7a:

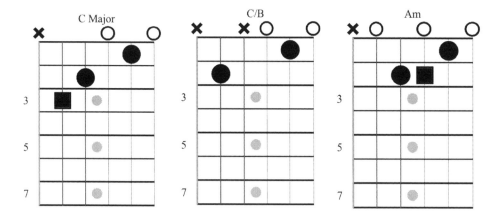

Be careful with the muted strings on these chords. It can work well to pick the bass note in each chord before strumming the rest of the strings.

The name C/B simply means that the C Major chord is being played over a B bass note. These *slash* chords normally sound a little strange out of context, but great when moving between two strong chords.

The same idea can be applied to the movement between G Major and Em7.

Example 7b:

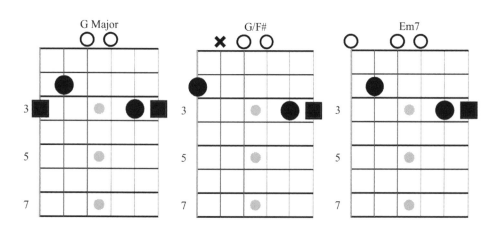

Check out the following examples to learn how you can use these slash chords to create moving basslines of your own. Experiment with other chord types.

Example 7c:

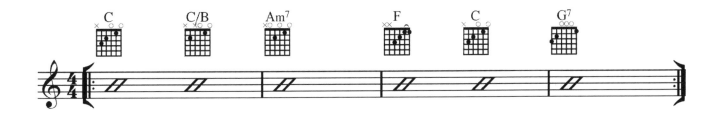

Example 7d:

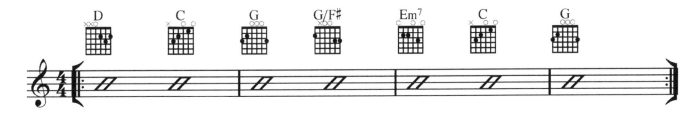

Chapter Eight: Basic Piano Voicings

The chords in the chapter are a little more suited for jazz guitar playing. This may not be your thing, but the rich texture of these chords is great to experiment with.

These voicings are called 'piano' voicings because they mimic the way many pianists voice chords on the piano. Notice that there is a one-string 'gap' between the bass note (sixth string) and the first upper-chord note (fourth string).

The underside of the first finger will be able to easily mute the unwanted string in the middle of the chord.

As always, use the steps in the **How to Practice** section to build your muscle memory and fluency with these chords. Then, add rhythm and start to combine them. Apply these voicings to the sequences at the end of this chapter, and also use them on the sequences in earlier chapters.

Example 8a:

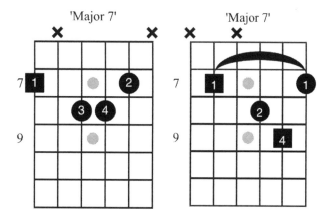

Example 8b:

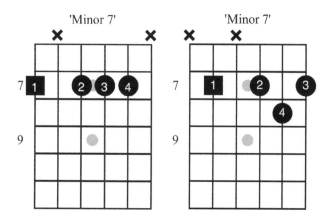

Example 8c:

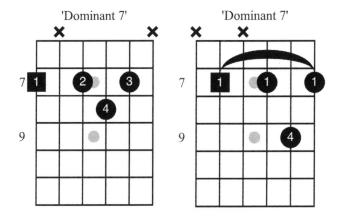

Example 8d:

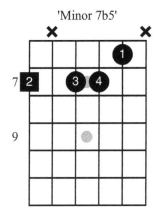

The following m7b5 shape is *technically* correct, but most guitarists will automatically reach for the second, easier voicing.

Example 8e:

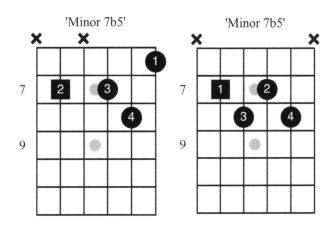

Test Yourself!

Play through the following progressions using piano voicing barre chords.

Example 8f:

Example 8g

Example 8h:

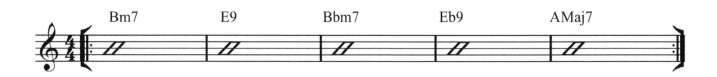

Example 8i:

Chapter Nine: Fourth-String Barres

In this short section, we will quickly look at how to play the most important chord-types on the top four strings. These voicings are used often in Motown and R&B music.

The first major voicing is a barre chord version of an open D Major chord. It's quite tricky to play, so most guitarists will miss out the root and play the chord with the same fingering as D Major.

Example 9a:

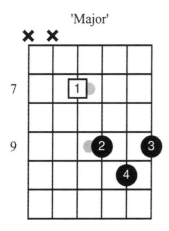

Once again, the Dm voicing is quite challenging, so try playing it without the root.

Example 9b:

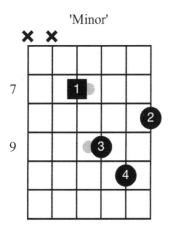

Example 9c:

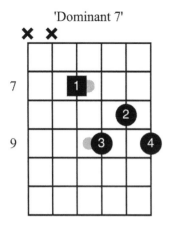

Example 9d:

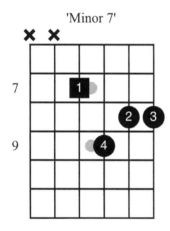

Some guitarists just use fingers one and three to play the following Maj7 barre chord. It's never worked for me, but it's a great option if you can manage it!

Example 9e:

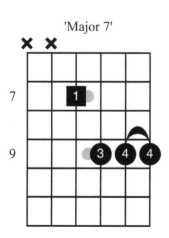

Notice how the following m7b5 chord is just like the top four notes of a '9' chord.

Example 9f:

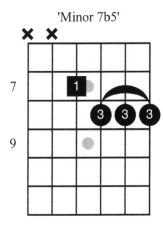

'Minor 7b5'

You'll need to know the notes on the fourth string so that you can place these movable voicings on the correct note.

Notes on the Fourth String

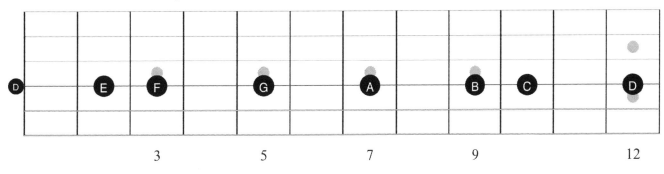

Test yourself!

Combine the chord voicings in this chapter with the ones from previous chapters to play through the following chord sequences.

Example 9g:

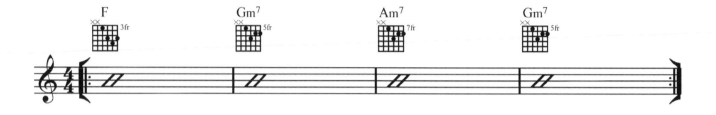

Example 9h:

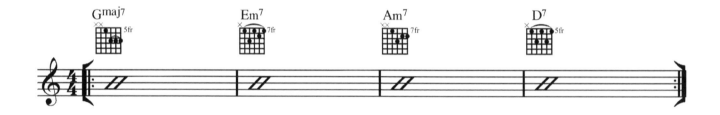

Example 9i:

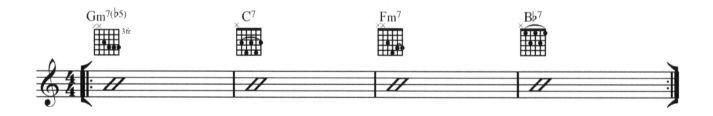

Come up with your own examples and use the four-string barres to play other sequences from earlier chapters.

Chapter Ten: Diatonic Extensions to Dominant 7 Chords

OK, I'll be honest… you probably don't need to work through the following two chapters unless you're really inquisitive about music, or you know that you definitely want to play jazz. If you want to strum out some pop songs, I recommend that you focus your time on the previous nine chapters and apply everything there to as many songs as you can. Spending time in the **How to Practice** and **Strumming** sections of this book will be much more beneficial to you than struggling through this section if you're not ready.

Find some band mates, rehearse, get a gig and have some fun.

However, if you want to peek into the murky underbelly of jazz, you may find the next two chapters interesting. They are advanced, so I really don't recommend them for beginners. Get out while you still can and come back later!

Still here?

OK then… The following section is taken from my best-selling book **Guitar Chords in Context**. It's a constant best seller on Amazon and goes way beyond being a simple chord dictionary. There's loads of stuff that we haven't covered in this book so I highly recommend it if you're interested in becoming a great guitarist.

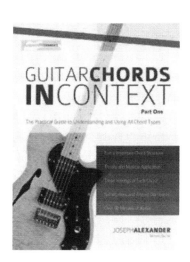

In jazz, it is common to add diatonic 'extensions' and chromatic 'alterations' to dominant 7 chords. A natural or 'diatonic' extension is a note that is added to the basic 1 3 5 b7 chord but lies within the original parent scale of the dominant chord. In other words, to form an extended dominant chord we continue skipping notes in the scale, just as we did when we originally learnt to form a chord.

We can extend the basic 1 3 5 b7 chord formula to include the 9th, 11th and 13th scale tones.

These extensions occur when we extend a scale beyond the first octave. For example, here is the parent scale of a C7 chord (C Mixolydian):

C	D	E	F	G	A	Bb	C	D	E	F	G	A	Bb	C
1	2	3	4	5	6	b7	**1/8**	9	**3**	11	**5**	13	**b7**	1

Notice that in the second octave, if a note is included in the original chord it is still referred to as 1, 3, 5, or b7. This is because the function of these notes never changes in the chord: A 3rd will always define whether a chord is major or minor and the b7 will always be an essential part of a m7 or 7 chord.

The notes *between* the chord tones are the notes that have changed their names. Instead of 2, 4 and 6, they are now 9, 11, and 13. These are called *compound* intervals

In very simple terms you could say that a C13 chord could contain *all* the intervals up until the 13th:

1 3 5 b7 9 11 and 13 – C E G Bb D F and A

In practice though, this is a huge amount of notes (we only have six strings), and playing that many notes at the same time produces an extremely heavy, undesirable sound where many of the notes clash with one another.

The answer to this problem is to remove some of the notes from the chord, but how do we know which ones?

There are no set rules about which notes to leave out in an extended chord, however, there *are* some guidelines about how to define a chord sound and what *does* need to be included.

To define a chord as major or minor, you must include some kind of 3rd.

To define a chord as dominant 7, major 7 or minor 7, you must include some kind of 7th.

These notes; the 3rds and 7ths, are called guide tones, and they are the most essential notes in any chord. It may surprise you, but these notes are more important than even the root of the chord and quite often in jazz rhythm guitar playing, the root of the chord is dropped entirely.

We will look more closely at guide tone or 'shell' chord voicings in the next chapter, but for now, we will examine common ways to play the extensions that regularly occur on dominant chords in jazz progressions.

To name a dominant chord, we always look to the highest extension that is included, so if the notes were 1, 3, b7, and 13, we would call this a dominant 13, or just '13' chord. Notice that it doesn't include the 5th, the 9th or the 11th, but it is still called a '13' chord.

As long as we have the 3rd and b7th, a chord will always be a dominant voicing.

We will begin by looking at a fairly common voicing of a D7 chord. In the following example, each *interval* of the chord is labelled in the diagram.

In D7 the intervals 1 3 5 b7 are the notes D, F#, A and C.

Example 10a:

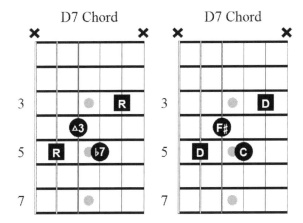

The 'triangle 3' symbol is shorthand for 'major 3rd'.

As you can see, this voicing of D7 doesn't include the 5th of the chord (A).

Here is the extended scale of D Mixolydian (the parent scale of D7).

D	E	F#	G	A	B	C	D	E	F#	G	A	B	C	D
1	2	3	4	5	6	b7	1/8	9	3	11	5	13	b7	1

We can use this voicing of D7 to form a dominant 9 or '9' chord. All we need to do is add the 9th of the scale (E) to the chord. The easiest way to do this is to move the higher-octave root (D) up by one tone and replace it with an E.

Example 10b:

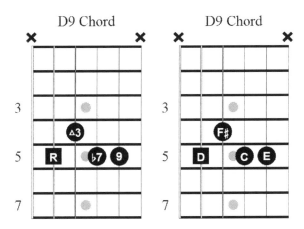

Look carefully to make sure you understand how I replaced the root of the chord with the 9th of the chord to form a dominant 9 or '9' chord.

The intervals contained in this chord voicing are now 1, 3, b7 and 9. We have the 1, 3 and b7 defining the chord as dominant and the 9th (E) creating the *extended* dominant 9th chord.

Dominant 11th or '11' chords are less common and need some special care because the major 3rd of the chord (F#) can easily clash with the 11th (G).

We will gloss over 11th chords for now and come back to them later, although the most common way to form an 11 chord it to lower the 5th of a dominant chord by a tone. The lowering of the 5th is generally voiced one octave above the 3rd, otherwise a semitone clash between the 3rd and 11th can occur.

Here is another voicing of a D7 chord, this time it does contain the 5th:

Example 10c:

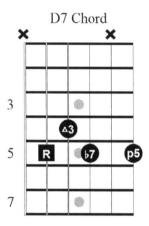

By lowering the 5th (A) by a tone to the 11th (G), we form a dominant 11 or '11' chord.

Example 10d:

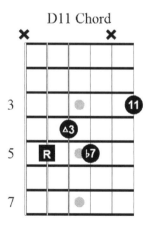

Dominant 13 chords are much more common in jazz than dominant 11 chords. They are normally created by raising the 5th of a dominant 7 chord by one tone so that it becomes the 13th (6th). It is common to include the 9th of the scale in a 13th chord, but it is by no means necessary.

By combining the last two ideas we can form a D9 chord with the fifth on the 1st string of the guitar:

Example 10e:

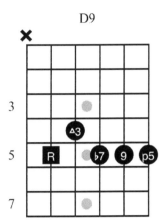

By raising the 5th by one tone, we can reach the 13th degree (interval) of the scale. The chord is given first with the intervals shown, and then with the recommended fingering:

Example 10f:

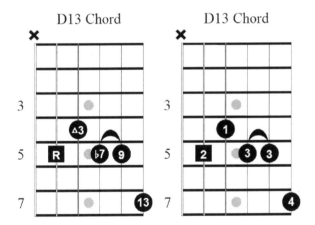

As I'm sure you're starting to see, adding extensions to dominant chords is simply a case of knowing where the desired extension is located on the fretboard and then moving a nonessential chord tone to that location.

The above 13 chord can also be voiced slightly differently to achieve a subtly different flavour. We could replace the 9th with the 3rd:

Example 10g:

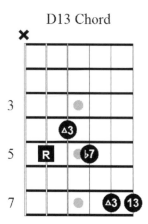

In this voicing, there are two 3rds which is completely acceptable. You will probably find the preceding version with the 9th included to be a slightly richer sound.

This approach can also be applied to a dominant 7 chord voiced from the 6th string of the guitar. Here is the root, 3 and b7 of a D7 chord with a 6th string root:

Example 10h:

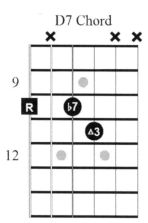

The 5th and higher octave root of this chord are located here:

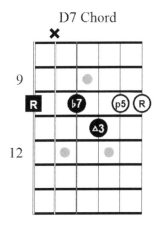

If you remember, we can raise the 5th by a tone to play the 13th of the chord, and we can raise the root of the chord by a tone to target the 9th.

Example 10i:

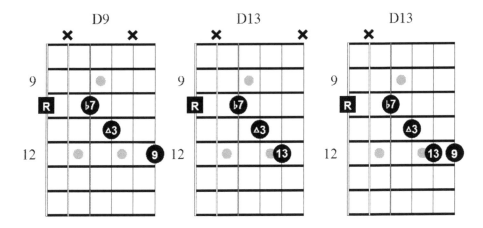

The third diagram shows a 13 chord which includes the 9th. It is still a 13th chord whether or not the 9th is present.

The following two 'shell' voicings are extremely useful fingerings to know, as it is easy to add extensions to them while keeping the root of the chord in the bass. However, as you will learn in chapter fourteen, diatonic extensions are often added by the clever use of chord *substitutions* that replace the original chord.

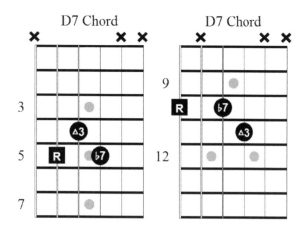

Chapter Eleven: Chromatic Alterations to Dominant Chords

While diatonic extensions (9, 11 and 13) are added to a dominant chord, it is also extremely common to add *altered* or *chromatic* extensions to a dominant chord. These alterations occur mainly at points of tension in a jazz progression, such as the dominant chord in a ii V I (two, five, one) sequence.

A chromatic alteration is a note that is added to a dominant chord that is not a 9, 11 or 13. We can account for *every* possible chromatic alteration by simply raising or flattening the 9th or 5th of the chord. In fact, there are only really four possible altered extensions; b5, #5, b9 and #9.

To see why this is true, let's look at a little bit of theory. Here is the two-octave scale of C Mixolydian, the parent scale of C7:

C	D	E	F	G	A	Bb	C	D	E	F	G	A	Bb	C
1	2	3	4	5	6	b7	1/8	9	3	11	5	13	**b7**	1

And here it is laid out on the guitar neck:

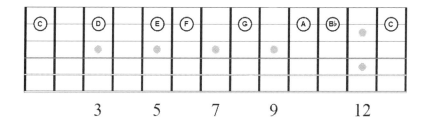

The 5th of the scale is the note G, and the 9th is the note D.

I can sharpen the 5th (G) to become a G# to create a #5 tension. I could also achieve the same result by flattening the 6th or 13th note (A) to become an Ab/G#.

For this reason, a b13 interval is exactly the same as a #5. The chords C7#5 and C7b13 are the same.

If you look at the fretboard again, you will see that a #11 (F#) is identical to a b5 (Gb).

A similar thing happens with the 9th of the scale however in any dominant chord you would *never* flatten the 3rd because it would change the quality of the chord from dominant to minor 7.

Remember dominant = 1 3 5 b7, and minor 7 = 1 b3 5 b7. By flattening the 3rd of a dominant chord, we change the chord quality so it is no longer dominant unless there is *another* major 3rd sounding in the chord.

I can sharpen the 9th (D) to become a D# and create a C7#9 sound. I can also flatten the 9th to Db to create a 7b9 sound.

Unlike the 3rd however, it is acceptable to remove the root note from any chord, so as you will see in chapter 9, it is possible to raise the root by a semitone to create a b9 sound.

We cannot raise the b7 of the chord because it would change the chord quality from dominant 7 to major 7.

In summary: b5 = #11 and #5 = b13 so the only true altered extensions to a dominant chord are b5, #5, b9 and #9. You will see chords written down like C7#11b13. This isn't wrong; it's just a question of terminology. The key is to realise that C7#9b13 is the same as C7#9#5.

The reason I teach b5, #5, b9, #9 is because it makes the chords much easier to understand and play on the fretboard.

We will work with a D7 chord to make these examples easier to play.

Here is a fretboard diagram showing the 1 3 b7 shell voicing of a dominant chord in black, and the 5th and 9th intervals marked in white:

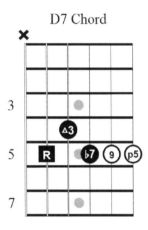

D7 Chord

I can create *any* altered extension by simply moving the white notes up or down by one semitone.

Example 11a:

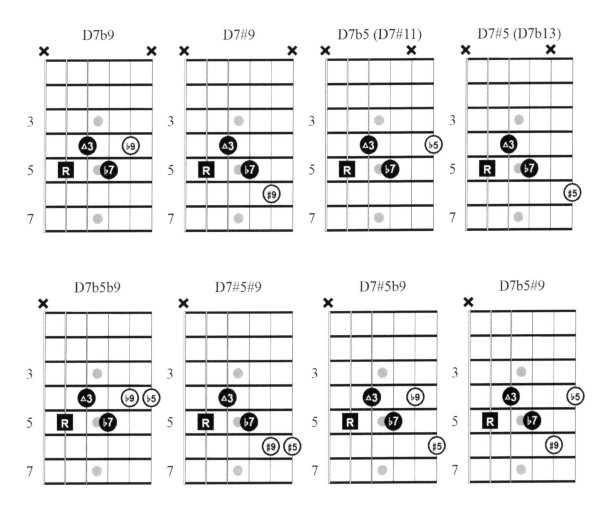

The same is true when we use the dominant 7 shell voicing with a root on the 6th string:

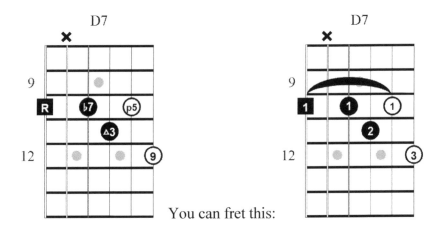

You can fret this:

Some of the altered extensions in this position can be a little hard to reach so quite often these voicings are played rootless. Here are a few of the altered extension permutations available in this position.

Example 11b:

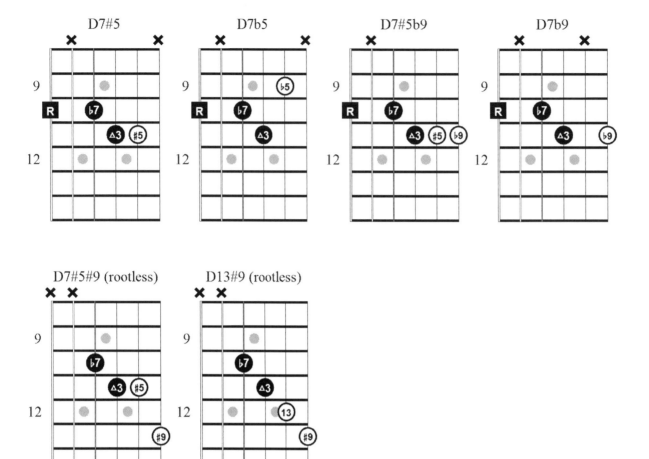

These approaches can be taken with a dominant 7 chord with the root on the 4th string too, although, in the basic root-position voicing we learnt earlier, we must omit the root when adding a #9 or b9.

The following example uses a G7 chord as the basis for the alterations.

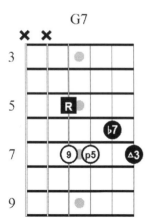

The easiest alterations to add are the #5 and b5, although often the root note will be raised a semitone to create a rootless 7b9 chord.

Example 11c:

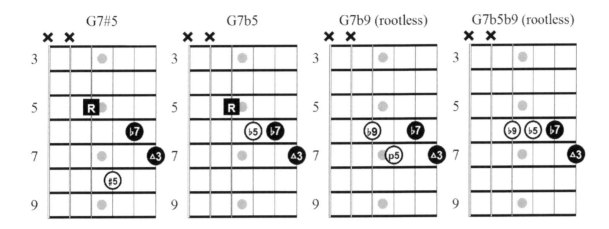

Quite often in jazz chord charts, you will simply see the symbol 'alt'. For example 'D7alt'. This means that the composer has not specified a particular altered extension for a dominant 7 chord and so you can use whichever one you feel works best with the music.

It is also important to know that just because a chord chart says '7' it doesn't mean that the chord must be played as a 'straight' 7 chord. If the dominant chord is *static* (not moving), it is normally fine to add in as many natural extensions as you like. For example, four bars of D7 could be played like this:

Example 11d:

If a dominant 7 chord is *functional* (resolving to another chord), then a basic '7' chord can normally be substituted for any dominant chord with a natural extension *or* chromatic alteration.

A chord progression like this:

Example 11e:

Could be played in any or more of the following ways:

Example 11f:

Example 11g:

Example 11h:

Try playing through the following examples beginning from different root notes, and substitute any diatonic or chromatic extensions you like for the dominant chords you have learned already.

1)

2)

3)

We can take the same approach when adding chromatic alterations to major 7, minor 7 and m7b5 chords; the secret is simply to know where the alterations are on the fretboard.

Chapter Twelve: How to Practice

In this section, I share my favourite techniques for learning and mastering new chords. I've been teaching these methods for years and I have broken them down into bullet point steps for you.

Learning New Open Chords.

The following set of steps is designed to help you quickly build the muscle memory that you need to memorise, recall and play any new open chord.

1) Read the chord diagram carefully! Ensure you're using the correct fingers on each note.

2) Place the tips of your fingers on the correct notes and strum the guitar once. Don't worry about the sound too much for now. Don't even worry too much about hitting the correct strings with the pick.

3) Remove your fretting hand from the guitar neck. Right off! Touch your leg with your fingertips.

4) Replace the fretting hand and fret the chord correctly. Strum the guitar. Don't worry about the sound.

5) Remove your hand again, right away from the guitar. Touch your leg again!

6) Replace your hand on the chord, and this time pick the correct strings one by one. Listen for any buzzes or muted notes and try adjusting your hand or thumb position until you can pick each note and it sounds clean. You may still get small buzzes at this stage, especially if you're a complete beginner. Don't worry! As your hand gets stronger, these buzzes will gradually disappear.

7) Lift your hand slightly from the guitar neck and replace the chord. You don't need to strum this time. Remove and replace the chord.

8) Remove and replace the chord.

9) Repeat steps 7 and 8.

10) Now try strumming the chord and check for buzzes.

11) If this is one of the first chords you're learning, then take a break. Get up, walk around and grab a drink.

12) Sit down again and repeat steps 1 – 11.

13) Finally, replace the chord on the neck and strum the strings. Listen. Remove, replace and strum the chord. Listen. Do this about ten times. If you know a few other chords, move on to the next set of steps immediately. If you don't know any other chords yet, repeat the above steps with a new chord. The first four chords I suggest you learn are Em, Am, C Major, then F Major 7.

Once you have a few (two or more) chords under your belt, the best thing you can do is to link them together. Our brains work well be learning information and movements in context. Want proof? What's easier to memorise, the words, "Quail, lemon, 78.4, Delhi," or the sentence, "The quail was drinking lemon in the 78.4-degree heat in Delhi."?

Most people would say the second sentence is more memorable because they can easily form a picture in their minds by linking up the words. All we did was add a little useful context.

When we learn chords individually, we are just creating a list of random words. When we link chords together, we learn the sounds and movements in context, so our brains will absorb them much more quickly.

Before you start, get a metronome. It's really important that you add an element of time keeping, and even a little 'time pressure' to get you moving more quickly. In music, rhythm is always king. Your audience will always notice a bad rhythm before noticing a bad note, so it pays to play in time from day one.

I recommend these metronomes.

Metrotimer for iPhone

Mobile Metronome for Android.

They both offer free versions, and it's great to finally be able to do something useful with a cell phone.

I'll use the chords of Em and Am for example, but you can pick any two chords you like. The best approach is to combine the new chord you are trying to learn with a simple chord you already know.

Learning Chords in Context

1) Complete steps 1 – 13 of the *Learning New Open Chords* method for each of the chords you wish to learn.

2) Set your metronome to 60 beats per minute (60 bpm).

3) Tap your foot and count "1, 2, 3, 4, 1, 2, 3, 4' in time with the click.

4) On a "1" strum an Em. Don't hold the chord! Immediately start moving to the next chord in the sequence (Am in this case). You are aiming to arrive there before the next "1", so you have four beats in which to get your fingers organised. If you get there early, just wait.

5) On the next "1" strum the Am.

Example 12a:

6) If you didn't make it, try again. If it's still tough, give yourself eight beats to get to the Am.

7) As soon as you strum the Am, start moving back to the Em so you can play it on the next "1". You don't need to let the chords ring. Just get moving!

8) If you arrive early at Em, wait and strum the chord on the next "1".

9) Don't worry about the sound of the chord, muted strings, buzzes, etc. These will improve with time. All you are concerned about is getting to the next chord by the next "1".

10) As you start to improve, repeat steps 4 – 8, but *keep moving!* Strum the guitar on the "1", and play whatever you have managed to get down in the fretting hand. It might sound terrible but that's not important right now. As soon as you have played one chord on beat one, immediately start moving to the next chord.

11) Take a break for two minutes.

12) Repeat step 10. If you're starting to get the idea, increase the metronome speed by 8bpm. Repeat.

13) As you improve, increase the metronome speed incrementally by around 8bpm until you get to around 120 bpm. Continue playing a down-strum on each chord on beat 1.

14) When you reach 120, stop, congratulate yourself, and set the metronome back on 60bpm. Repeat all the previous steps, but now allow each chord to last for just two beats. It will *feel* different, but you are playing the same speed as you were before. Two strums per bar at 60 bpm = one strum at 120 bpm.

You should now be playing Em on beat 1 and 3 and then Am on beats 1 and 3. Again, if this is too difficult then slow the metronome down slightly. As ever, don't worry too much about the sound of the chords, the goal is to be in the right place at the right time.

Example 12b:

16) Once again, gradually increase the metronome speed, but this time by 4bpm until you reach 120bpm, or wherever you simply can't make it anymore.

Repeat the previous process but now play four strums on each chord. It's OK if you slow right down for this but keep the metronome ticking.

Example 12c:

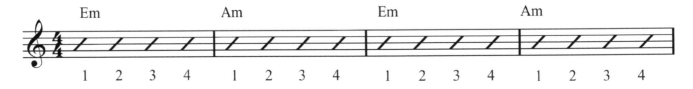

17) Introduce some rhythms using the method in the next chapter. Ensure that whatever rhythm you choose has a 1/4 note on beat four so that you have time to change between chords.

The above process can be used to learn, and also introduce any new chord into your vocabulary. Don't worry too much about the way each chord sounds; the idea is to build confident muscle memory first and then hone the movement a little later once you can confidently finger the chord.

Chapter Thirteen: Adding Rhythm

The following section is taken from my book, Beginner's Guitar Lessons: The Essential Guide

I make clear to all my private students that I am not a 'theory first' teacher. I prefer to get hands-on and have them making music as soon as possible. The one exception to this is in the way I teach rhythm and strumming.

Your strumming hand (normally your right if you're right-handed) only has two useful directions to hit the strings; *up* and *down.* When you understand why certain strums are *ups* and others are *downs,* you build a fundamental security with rhythm. In fact, if you practice the following method, quite soon you'll never wonder how to play a rhythm again. You'll simply hear it and replicate it instantly and unconsciously.

When we talk about rhythm in music, what we're essentially doing is breaking down a song into little chunks. That song might be a 3 minute Beatles tune or a 17 minute Rachmaninov symphony. Either way, we always arrange the chunks of rhythm the same way.

You may have heard the words *bars* and *beats* before. A beat is one pulse of a song: the distance from one click to the next on your metronome. Think of the beat as a one-syllable word.

One beat of a piece of music looks like this:

This note is called a **'Quarter Note'** as you can fit four of them in a bar, i.e., four ¼ notes = 1 bar.

A bar is a *container* for the beats, and at this stage, we will normally have four beats in each bar. An empty bar of music looks like this:

The 4/4 at the start tells us that there are 4 beats in the bar.

If we fill the bar with quarter notes it looks like this:

This is a whole load of preamble to get to one very simple rule:

Every time you see a ♩, you play a down strum.

Down strums are always on the beat, so if you're counting 1, 2, 3, 4 as in previous chapters, every time you say a number you strum downwards on guitar.

Look at and listen to **Example 13a:**

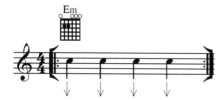

Set your metronome to play at 60 beats per minute, then play a down strum on each click while holding down the chord of E minor.

Try the same idea with A minor:

Example 13b:

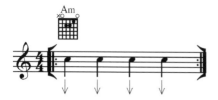

While this is a great method for developing good solid rhythm, music would be extremely dull if all our rhythms were like this.

One way to add interest is to double up on each quarter (1/4) note. In other words, imagine splitting each 1/4 note in half. This gives us 8 notes in the bar, and these are imaginatively called *1/8* or *eighth* notes.

On its own, an 1/8th note looks like this:

But when we put two of them next to each other, we join up their tails:

In other words, in music, instead of seeing two 1/8th notes written like this:

, you would always see them written like this: .

You can see that two 1/8th notes take the same amount of time to play as one 1/4 note. So

takes the same amount of time to play as,

That is the end of the mathematics; I promise!

As you can see in the previous example, when we play 1/8th notes, our down strum is still in exactly the same place. All we need to do is squeeze in an up strum between each one. This up-strum should be *exactly* in the middle of each down.

On paper it looks like this:

Example 13c:

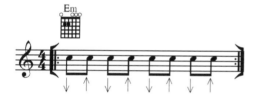

Set your metronome to 60 beats per minute and begin by playing just a down strum on each click. When you're ready, add up strums in the middle of each down. Count out loud '1 and 2 and 3 and 4 and ', etc.

Listen to the audio example to help you.

Try the same idea with other chords like D Major, shown below.

Example 13d:

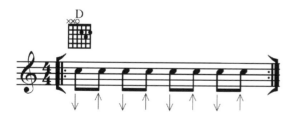

While we have added interest to our playing by adding more strums, music would be very repetitive if this was the only rhythm we ever played. To add interest, let's learn to combine 1/4 notes and 1/8th notes to add variety.

Look at **Example 13e:**

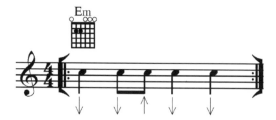

Beat 1 is a down strum, **beat 2** is a 'down-up', **beat 3** is a down strum, as is **beat 4.**

Before you play, set the metronome on 60 bpm and say out loud:

One. Two and Three. Four. Down. Down-Up Down. Down.

Say it in time, rhythmically and confidently. Saying the rhythm out loud really helps your brain to process what it needs to do to strum the rhythm in time.

When you're ready, strum the rhythm confidently. Don't worry about any buzzes in your fretting hand. Ignore them; we're only focusing on strumming.

When you're happy with the above, try the next idea.

Example 13f:

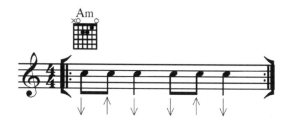

Say out loud *"One and Two. Three and Four. Down Up Down. Down Up Down."*

If it helps, you might want to think *jin gle bells jin gle bells.*

Throughout any rhythm you play on the guitar, the strumming hand never stops moving. It is constantly moving up and down in time. Downward movements are on the beats, upward movements are between the beats. This keeps you in time; like a little built-in conductor. To create rhythms, all we do is sometimes hit the strings and sometimes miss them.

Here are some other rhythms to practice:

Example 13g:

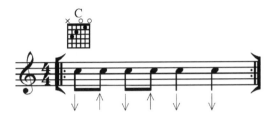

Down-Up Down-Up Down. Down.

Example 13h:

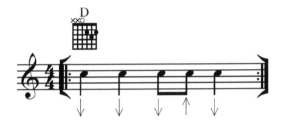

Down. Down. Down-Up Down.

With each rhythm, remember to keep your strumming hand moving down and up all the time. To play a 1/4 note, simply don't strike the guitar on the up-strum.

More Interesting Rhythms

The simplest and most common way to add energy to your rhythm playing is to miss out strumming some down beats. To teach you this idea, we need to introduce a new musical symbol. It is an 1/8th note *rest* and looks like this: ⁊

This rest simply means *silence* or 'don't strum.' It will always be seen in combination with a strummed quarter note so that together they add up to **one beat,** like this: ⁊ ♪

Before, when we played the rhythm ♪♪, the strumming pattern was **Down Up.** With the rhythm ⁊ ♪ , we *miss out the down strum* but *still play the up strum*.

To make this easier, always keep moving the strumming hand as if you are going to play the down strum, but simply *miss the strings.* This will keeps you in time.

In other words, the strumming hand is going up and down constantly, but *does not make contact* with the strings on the down strum. This is shown in the notation below by the brackets around the arrow.

To practice this idea, study the following.

Example 13i:

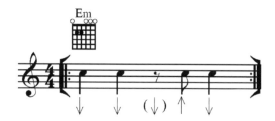

Count out loud: "Down. Down. Miss Up Down".

Next, try holding down an E minor chord while you strum this rhythm. Remember to keep the strumming hand moving all the time, miss the strings on the down strum of **beat 3** but make contact on up strum of **beat '3 and'.**

This is tricky at first, but incredibly important.

Once you have this idea under your fingers, try the next rhythm:

Example 13j:

Down. Down Up Miss Up Down.

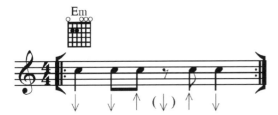

Finally, strum this:

Example 13k:

Down. Miss Up Miss Up Down.

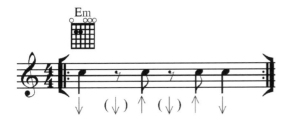

When you're comfortable with the idea of missing a down strum, transfer these rhythms to some of the chord changes given in the early chapters. There is no need to make the tasks difficult for both hands at the same time.

Try the following at 60 beats per minute.

Example 3l:

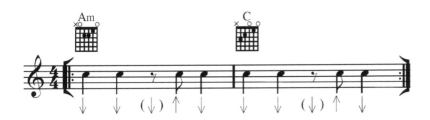

Here's one more example to spur your imagination. Spend as much time as you can mixing and matching chord changes and rhythms.

Example 13m:

Down Up Miss Up Miss Up Down.

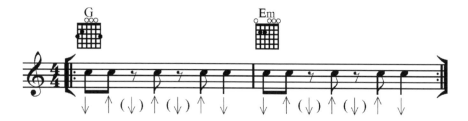

Now try making up some of your own rhythms and apply them to simple chord changes.

Conclusion and Practice Directions

There's a huge amount of information in this book, and there is probably a temptation to try to memorise it all at once. I strongly advise against this, and instead suggest you try to learn just one or two chords a day (or even a week). Spend the majority of your practice time exploring and actually using these chords and voicings.

Remember, context is everything. There's no point learning a long list of information if you're never going to figure out when to play it or what effect it has on the music. While chords can easily be substituted (a Dominant 9 for a Dominant 7, for example), the effect caused by these small changes can be quite dramatic.

In theory, '6' chords function in exactly the same way as straight-ahead Major chords, but you're really going to want to know what that substitution will do to the song. Experimentation is the key (and rehearsal with your band too), because the last thing they need is to hear a 'strange' note appear while they're playing. Sometimes risks are good, but normally it's best to try out these ideas with your band *before* you get on stage!

My biggest piece of advice is that there's no massive hurry to learn everything, especially the information in Chapters Ten and Eleven. Those ideas really are quite advanced and I've only included them here for completeness and to give you a deeper understanding of how chord theory works.

If you're interested in what my first guitar lesson looks like for the average beginner, in an hour I would normally have expected to cover five or six chords (Em, Am, C Major, F Major7, D Major and G Major), taught them the steps in Chapter Twelve, and taught them how to strum the first basic rhythms in Chapter Thirteen.

The real work, however, begins once they get home.

I insist that my students practice for a minimum of 20 minutes a day, ideally 20 minutes twice a day because the physical repetition is important to build muscle memory. Their homework is to practice the steps I've given in Chapters Twelve and Thirteen.

If the student practices every day, then normally they come back to me the following week to get some more chords, a few songs, and some more rhythms to work on.

Often, my students develop an effortless command of the chords in Chapters One and Two after about four weeks.

If they've practiced well, the continuing improvement in their ability is exponential because they've covered the basics so thoroughly. At this point, I can write down almost any new chord and they will grasp it quickly. The muscle memory work has paid off by this stage, so all I need to do to teach them an actual song is to write down the chord sequence and strumming pattern (rhythm).

There's no great secret to learning how to play a musical instrument; it's simply a case of committing yourself and practicing regularly. The hardest part is making a lifestyle change to fit in some quality guitar practice time.

Add up all the time you spend on Facebook, Twitter, Instagram, playing video games, watching cat videos on YouTube etc. Reduce that time by 20 minutes and play your guitar instead. I promise you, it's much more rewarding than worrying what Kim and Kanye are up to. Your soul will thank you.

If you need any further help with learning guitar, there are loads of good resources out there.

JustinGuitar is an amazing resource for beginners and improvers alike. He's got a lesson on pretty much any song you care to learn, and his patient, upbeat style is a joy to learn from.

For more detailed information for beginners, check out the following book. It contains everything you need to know to become a competent guitarist. After workign through it, you'll be comfortable with chords, picking, strumming and chord progressions.

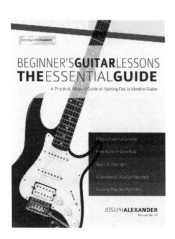

Chords are a huge subject and I go into great detail in Guitar Chords in Context. In this book you'll learn much more about voicings and how to use chords to open up the guitar neck. Three voicings of each chord type are given and you'll learn everything about how chords are created, used and applied.

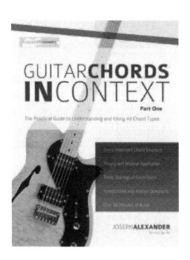

I really hope you enjoy your journey as a guitarist.

Have fun, and keep rocking!

Joseph

Get a Free Book!

If you're enjoying this book, please take a second to write a review on Amazon. If you email us a link to your review at webcontact@fundamental-changes.com **we will send you a free book of your choice from the following list of titles:**

25 Blues Scale Licks for Blues Guitar

25 Major Pentatonic Licks for Blues Guitar

25 Major ii V I Licks for Jazz Guitar

or

Drop 2 Voicings for Jazz and Modern Guitar

Just let us know which one you want!

Other Best-Selling Guitar Books from Fundamental Changes

Each book includes:

- Over 100 Pages of expert, professional tuition

- Around 150 examples in standard notation and tab

- Accompanying audio downloads that you can get for free from **www.fundamental-changes.com**

www.fundamental-changes.com also includes over **250 free guitar lessons**, many of which have HD video. We add new lessons all the time so keep checking back to improve your playing for free.

Have fun,

Joseph

Made in the USA
Lexington, KY
10 November 2017